MACMILL
INTERME

CHARLES DICKENS

Oliver Twist

Retold by Margaret Tarner

2 CD DISKS AT

BACK

Library

MACMILLAN

Ca~~mden School for Girls~~

London NW5 2DB

INTERMEDIATE LEVEL

Founding Editor: John Milne

The Macmillan Readers provide a choice of enjoyable reading materials for learners of English. The series is published at six levels – Starter, Beginner, Elementary, Pre-intermediate, Intermediate and Upper.

Level control
Information, structure and vocabulary are controlled to suit the students' ability at each level.

The number of words at each level:

Starter	about 300 basic words
Beginner	about 600 basic words
Elementary	about 1100 basic words
Pre-intermediate	about 1400 basic words
Intermediate	about 1600 basic words
Upper	about 2200 basic words

Vocabulary
Some difficult words and phrases in this book are important for understanding the story. Some of these words are explained in the story and some are shown in the pictures. From Pre-intermediate level upwards, words are marked with a number like this: ...³. These words are explained in the Glossary at the end of the book.

19434

Contents

A Note About the Author

Charles Dickens is one of the greatest English writers. He was born near Portsmouth in the south of England on 7th February 1812.

Charles Dickens' father worked in an office. John Dickens did not earn much money and the family could not pay their bills. When Charles Dickens was 12 years old, John Dickens and his family went to prison because they could not pay their bills. Charles did not go to prison. He went to work in a factory. He had to work many hours each day. He had to stick labels onto bottles. Charles Dickens was very unhappy at this time. He never forgot about his life at the factory.

In 1821, when he was 15 years old, Dickens went to work in an office. He was not paid much money but he had many friends.

In 1833, Charles Dickens started writing stories. He became very famous and very rich. *Oliver Twist*, the story of a poor boy without a family was published in 1838. Other famous books by Charles Dickens are: *A Christmas Carol* (1843), *Bleak House* (1853), *A Tale of Two Cities* (1859), *Great Expectations* (1861) and *Our Mutual Friend* (1864).

Dickens knew how the poor people lived in England. Many of his stories are about poor people. Dickens was angry when he found out how poor children lived. The children were often hungry and they were beaten.

Charles Dickens died on 9th June 1870. He was 58 years old. Dickens is buried in the famous church, Westminster Abbey, in London.

A Note About England in the Nineteenth Century

Dickens' story, *Oliver Twist*, takes place in London in the 1830s. At this time, Great Britain was a very rich country and London was the largest city in Europe. Many rich people lived in London. They had expensive houses and they had the very best food and drink. They travelled in fine carriages pulled by horses and they wore beautiful and fashionable clothes.

When he lived in London, Charles Dickens saw the rich people living in beautiful houses. However, most people in England at this time did not have much money. Thousands of poor people lived in London. They lived in small, dirty houses and did not have enough to eat. They had no work and many men, women and children became criminals. At this time, a criminal could be hanged for murdering somebody or for stealing. If somebody was hanged they had a rope pulled tight around their neck to kill them.

England is divided into counties and each county is divided into parishes. In the nineteenth century, the officials of the parish had to look after the poor people who did not have homes to live in and food to eat.

In the nineteenth century, a workhouse was built in every parish. Workhouses were places where the poor people were made to live. Workhouses were usually terrible places. The poor people who lived in them were given food to eat and beds to sleep in. But they were made to work very hard in the workhouses and the food was very bad.

The men in charge of workhouses were called masters. Matrons were the women who helped look after the women and children in the workhouses. Another official who worked for the parish was called the beadle. A beadle wore special clothes and carried a special stick. His job was to punish people who had done wrong.

Prologue

The baby began to cry. The baby's young mother opened her eyes. She tried to lift her head from the pillow. The baby was three minutes old and it was crying for the first time.

'Give me my baby,' the girl whispered.

The doctor walked to the bed. He put the child into the mother's arms.

The girl gave a sigh[1] and then she spoke.

'Look after my child,' she whispered. Then the poor girl closed her eyes – for the last time.

The doctor spoke to the matron[2] of the parish workhouse[3], Mrs Corney.

'Well, Mrs Corney,' the doctor said, 'the parish workhouse must look after the orphan[4] child. It's weak and it might die. Do you know the dead mother's name?'

'We know nothing about her,' Mrs Corney answered. 'She was found yesterday. She had fallen in the street.'

'No name and no wedding ring[5],' the doctor said sadly. He left the room.

Mrs Corney looked at the dead girl. There was something round the girl's neck. It was a shining gold locket[6] on a chain.

The matron took the chain off the girl's neck. She held the locket in her hand.

'She has no use for this now,' Mrs Corney said softly. And she put the locket and chain in her pocket.

1
Early Days

The orphan boy did not die. And Mr Bumble gave him a name.

Mr Bumble was the parish beadle[7]. He gave all the orphans names when they arrived in the workhouse. He named them using the letters of the alphabet. T was the next letter. So Mr Bumble named the child Twist – Oliver Twist.

Oliver was now eleven years old. He was a pale, thin child. All the workhouse children were thin and ill. They were always hungry.

The boys were fed three times a day. But all they got to eat was a small bowl of gruel[8]. Three small bowls of gruel were not enough. The hungry boys were desperate[9]. They had a meeting and made a decision. One of them must ask for more food. The boys chose Oliver Twist!

Evening came. The boys stood in a line in the long, stone hall. They waited for their bowls of gruel. They ate very quickly. In a moment, every bowl was empty. All the boys looked at Oliver.

Oliver was very afraid. But he was also very hungry. Carrying his bowl, he walked up to the master of the workhouse. Oliver looked up at the man and spoke.

'Please, sir, I want some more,' he whispered.

'What did you say?' the master said in surprise.

'Please, sir, I want some more,' Oliver repeated.

The master gave a great shriek[10]. He took hold of Oliver by the collar of his thin shirt.

'Get the beadle! Bring Mr Bumble here!' the master shouted in anger.

In a few minutes, Mr Bumble hurried in. He was a bad-

'Please, sir, I want some more,' Oliver whispered.

tempered big, fat man. He wore a big hat and carried a long, thin stick.

'Well, what's the matter?' Mr Bumble asked angrily.

'Oliver Twist has asked for more!' the master cried.

'Asked for more?' Mr Bumble repeated. He glared[11] at Oliver. 'He's asking us for more! This boy is bad, very bad. One day he'll be hanged[12]. Give him to me!'

Then Mr Bumble took hold of Oliver. He beat the poor child with his stick. When the beadle was tired, he threw Oliver onto the ground.

'Lock the boy in a dark room!' he shouted. 'Then he must leave the workhouse. He can't stay here. He will be sold as an apprentice[13].'

The next day, a notice was put up outside the workhouse.

PARISH BOY FOR SALE
£5 will be paid to anyone who will take
a parish boy as an apprentice.

———

Oliver sat in the dark room in the cellar. He was cold, hungry and afraid.

If I stay here, I'll die, he thought. But a new master may kill me. I'll run away!

The night was cold and dark. Oliver climbed carefully out of a small window. He hurried along the quiet streets.

There was a large stone outside the town. On it was written, LONDON – 10 MILES.

'Mr Bumble won't find me in London,' Oliver said to himself. 'I'll get work there, I'm sure.'

So Oliver started to walk. He walked for seven days. Sometimes he begged[14] for food. Most of the time, he was hungry.

At last, Oliver reached Barnet, a town near London. But he

was too hungry and exhausted to go on. He sat down by the side of the road.

A strange-looking boy was standing on the other side of the road. The boy had a small nose that turned up at the end and a very dirty face. He wore a man's coat which was far too big for him. His old hat was on the back of his head. The boy stood there, with his hands in his pockets. He stared at Oliver with his sharp little eyes.

At last, he walked over to Oliver and spoke.

'Hallo. What's the matter with you?' the strange boy asked.

Oliver began to cry.

'I'm very tired. And I'm very hungry,' he said.

'Hungry?' the boy repeated. 'I'll buy you some food. Come with me.'

A few minutes later, Oliver was eating bread and meat.

The strange boy watched Oliver eating. Then he spoke again.

'My friends call me the Artful Dodger,' the boy said. 'Are you going to London?'

'Yes, I am,' Oliver replied.

'Got any place to sleep? Any money?' the Dodger asked.

'No,' Oliver answered sadly. 'Do you live in London?'

'Yes, I do. And I'm going there tonight,' the Dodger replied. 'I know an old gentleman there. He'll give you a place to sleep.'

'Oh, thank you, thank you,' Oliver said.

When it was dark, the two boys began walking to London. At eleven o'clock, they reached the great city.

The Dodger led Oliver along narrow, dirty streets. The streets were full of poorly-dressed people. The noise and the darkness made Oliver very afraid.

Suddenly, the Dodger stopped. He opened a door and whistled[15].

It was very dark inside the house. The Dodger pulled Oliver

up the broken stairs. He opened a door and then pushed Oliver into a dark and dirty room.

2

At Fagin's

The walls of the room were black with dirt.. There was a table near the fire. On the table was a bottle, with a lighted candle in it.

A very old man was standing near the fire. He turned quickly as the two boys came into the room.

The old man had a beard and his face was ugly and wrinkled[16]. On his head was a hat and his long, dirty red hair hung down his back. He stared at Oliver with his bright, dark eyes.

There were four or five boys in the room. They were sitting on old sacks[17]. The boys got up and came and stood close to the Dodger. He whispered a few words to the old man. Then the Dodger spoke in a louder voice.

'Fagin, this is my new friend, Oliver Twist,' the Dodger said.

The old man smiled at Oliver.

'Very pleased to see you, Oliver, my dear,' the old man said. 'Come nearer to the fire, my boy.'

Oliver stared round the dirty room. There was a rope tied across one corner of the room. Many brightly-coloured silk handkerchiefs[18] were hanging over the rope.

Fagin smiled again.

'My handkerchiefs are pretty, aren't they, Oliver?' he said. 'And they're all waiting to be washed!'

To Oliver's surprise, all the boys laughed.

Supper was ready. Soon everyone was eating and drinking.

Fagin gave Oliver a strong, hot drink.

'Drink this, Oliver, my boy,' the old man said.

Oliver drank. Suddenly, he felt very sleepy. Someone lifted him onto some old sacks. Immediately Oliver fell asleep.

———

Oliver woke up late the next morning. The boys were not there. But Fagin was sitting at the table. In front of him was an open box.

The old man took a gold watch from the box. He looked at it and smiled. One by one, he held up rings, chains and jewels. Very carefully, he put each one back in the box.

Suddenly, Fagin turned. He grabbed[19] a knife from the table and stood up quickly. Fagin glared at Oliver.

'Why are you watching me?' the old man cried. 'Did you see my pretty things?'

'Yes, sir. I'm very sorry, sir,' Oliver replied. He was shaking with fear.

Fagin laughed and put down the knife.

'These pretty things are for my old age,' the old man said. 'I'm keeping them so I'll have some money when I'm old. You won't say anything to the others, will you, my boy?'

'Oh no, sir,' Oliver replied.

'Then get up now,' Fagin said. 'Get washed. There's water in a bowl by the door.'

Oliver walked to the door. When he turned back, the box of gold and jewels was gone.

Some time later, the Dodger returned. A boy called Charley Bates was with him. Fagin, Oliver, the Dodger and Charley sat down to eat a breakfast of bread, meat and coffee.

'I hope you've worked hard this morning,' Fagin said to the boys. 'What have you got, Dodger?'

The Dodger gave Fagin two wallets[20].

'Good,' the old man said with a smile. 'Very nicely made, Dodger. What have you got, Charley?'

Charley gave Fagin four silk handkerchiefs.

'Very nice, Charley, very nice,' Fagin said. 'We'll teach you to make handkerchiefs, Oliver. Would you like that?'

'Very much, sir,' Oliver replied.

The boys laughed.

And now, Fagin and the boys played a very strange game. First, Fagin put handkerchiefs, silver boxes and other things in his pockets. Then he walked up and down the room.

Sometimes, the old man stopped and looked around. Sometimes, he touched his pockets. The two boys followed close behind him. When Fagin stopped, they stopped. When the old man looked round, the boys hid behind him.

Oliver laughed and laughed. He thought this was a very good game!

At last, the boys got nearer to Fagin. Quickly and quietly, they took everything from his pockets. Then the game started all over again.

———

In the afternoon a young woman came in. Her name was Nancy. She had long hair, and make-up on her face. She was dressed in very brightly-coloured clothes. Oliver thought she was kind and friendly.

After a time, Fagin gave the Dodger some money. Then Charley, the Dodger and Nancy went out.

Fagin smiled at Oliver. 'They've gone out to enjoy themselves, my dear,' the old man said. 'Work hard here and you'll enjoy yourself too.'

Then Fagin smiled again.

'Is my handkerchief coming out of my pocket, Oliver?' the old man asked.

'Yes, sir,' Oliver replied.

'Try to take it out, Oliver,' Fagin said. Then he turned away.

*Oliver laughed and laughed. He thought this was
a very good game!*

Very carefully, Oliver took the handkerchief from Fagin's pocket.

'Have you taken it?' the old man asked.

'Yes, sir. Here it is!' Oliver replied.

'You're a clever boy, Oliver!' Fagin cried. 'You'll be as good as the Dodger one day!'

Oliver was pleased. But he did not understand the old man's words.

3

Stop Thief!

The Dodger, Charley and the other boys went out every morning. Oliver stayed with Fagin. But the little boy had a job too. He worked on the silk handkerchiefs. All the handkerchiefs had letters stitched onto them. Oliver had to cut these stitches from the silk handkerchiefs very carefully.

For three days, the boys came back with nothing. Fagin was very angry. He shouted at the Dodger. He tried to push Charley downstairs.

The next day, Fagin sent Oliver out with the other boys.

The Dodger and Charley walked very slowly along the crowded streets. Oliver was afraid they would all be late for work.

The boys walked on. They went up a narrow street and into a square[21].

There were stalls and shops selling books on one side of the square. At one of the stalls, an old gentleman was looking at the books. He picked one up and began to read.

The Dodger stopped. 'He'll do,' he said quietly.

'Right,' Charley whispered.

The two boys walked across the square. Oliver followed.

15

The old gentleman went on reading. He had grey hair and wore gold spectacles. He wore a long, dark green coat and white trousers.

The Dodger moved nearer. The next moment, the old gentleman's silk handkerchief was in the Dodger's hand. The Dodger and Charley ran and hid in the doorway of a house.

The old gentleman touched his pocket. He turned round quickly. He saw Oliver standing behind him.

'That boy's got my handkerchief!' the old gentleman cried.

Oliver turned and ran.

'Stop thief! Stop thief!' the gentleman shouted. He began to run after Oliver.

The Dodger and Charley began to shout too.

'Stop thief! Stop thief!'

In a few moments, a hundred people were shouting. A hundred people were running after Oliver. Oliver was terrified. He ran faster and faster, stumbled and fell to the ground.

The poor boy looked up at the angry faces above him.

A policeman pushed his way through the crowd of people. 'Is this the boy?' he asked.

'Yes, I'm afraid so,' the old gentleman said sadly.

'No, no, it wasn't me, sir! It was two other boys, sir!' poor Oliver cried.

The policeman laughed. He took hold of Oliver's collar. 'Get up!' he said. 'Get up and come with me!'

But another man was pushing his way through the crowd.

'Stop! That's not the boy. I saw what happened,' he cried.

'I am the owner of the bookstall,' the man went on. 'I saw three boys in the square. One of the other boys took the handkerchief. This boy did nothing.'

The policeman let go of Oliver. The poor child fell to the ground again. His face was very white.

'The boy is ill!' the old gentleman with gold spectacles cried. 'Call a cab[22], someone. The boy's coming home with me.'

'Stop! That's not the boy. I saw what happened,'
the man cried.

The cab arrived. Oliver was put gently inside it. The old gentleman got in and shouted his address to the driver. Then the cab moved away.

———

Fagin was waiting for the boys to return. He was worried. They had been away for a long time.

Then he heard footsteps on the stairs. 'Only two of them,' he said.

The door opened. Charley and the Artful Dodger came in slowly.

'Where's Oliver, you young dogs?' Fagin cried. He grabbed the Dodger round the neck.

'What's happened to the boy?' the old man shouted. 'Tell me quickly, or I'll kill you!'

The Dodger's face went red and he coughed. 'He went with the old gentleman,' the Dodger gasped.

'What old gentleman?' Fagin shrieked.

'The old gentleman we stole a handkerchief from,' the boy replied. 'They went off in a cab. The old gentleman told the driver to go to Pentonville.'

With a cry of anger, Fagin pushed the Dodger across the room. Then he hit Charley on the head.

At the same moment, the door opened. A young man came in, followed by Nancy.

'What's the matter, you old thief?' the young man cried. 'Beating the boys again, are you? One day they'll murder you!'

'Hush, Bill, hush!' Fagin whispered. 'Don't say that word here.'

Bill Sikes laughed. Sikes was a heavy young man, dressed in very dirty clothes. He had a large, dirty face. His small eyes were very cruel.

A dirty white dog followed Sikes into the room. The animal

went to the other side of the room and lay down in a corner.

Sikes sat down at the table. 'Bring us a drink, Fagin,' he said, 'and tell me what the shouting is about.'

Fagin told Sikes about Oliver.

'It's bad, Bill,' the old man said. 'The boy may tell the old gentleman all about us.'

Sikes laughed again. 'If he does, and the gentleman tells the police, you'll be hanged!' he replied.

'There'll be trouble for you too, Bill,' said Fagin. 'People know that we work together.'

The two men stared at one another. Then Sikes turned away.

'We'll get the boy back,' Sikes said. 'Someone must look for him.'

Fagin nodded. Then he smiled. 'Nancy, my dear, you can go,' he said.

Nancy shook her head. 'I don't want anything to do with it,' she said quietly.

'Oh, yes you do!' Sikes said. He grabbed the girl roughly by the arm.

'You'll go, Nancy – I say you will. Or you won't go anywhere again,' he said.

'Yes, Nancy must go,' Fagin added. 'But wait, my dear. I have some new clothes for you.'

Nancy put on a white apron and a straw hat.

'Here's a basket to carry,' Fagin said. 'Now you look like an honest young woman.

'Go to Pentonville,' Fagin went on. 'Ask people questions about Oliver. Remember, the boy must be found!'

Nancy laughed. She began to walk up and down the room. Suddenly she looked sad and spoke in a strange voice.

'I have lost my little brother, Oliver,' she said softly. 'Do you know where he is? I must take him home!'

'Very good, Nancy, very good!' Fagin cried. 'Start now. Go to Pentonville every day until you find the boy!'

19

4

Oliver Finds a Friend

Oliver was in a quiet, clean room. He was lying on a big, soft bed with clean sheets and pillows. He looked around the room in surprise.

'Where am I?' Oliver whispered.

A kind-looking woman was standing by the bed.

'This is Mr Brownlow's house and I am his housekeeper[23],' the woman said. 'You have been very ill. But you are getting better now.'

A little later, the old gentleman with gold spectacles came into the room. He looked down at Oliver.

'How do you feel, my boy?' Mr Brownlow asked.

'Very, very happy, sir,' Oliver replied. 'Thank you for bringing me here.'

As the child spoke, his eyes closed again. Soon he was fast asleep. Mr Brownlow went to sit in his library.

There was a painting of a beautiful young girl hanging on one of the walls. Mr Brownlow sat and stared at the face of the girl in the portrait.

'That's strange,' Mr Brownlow said to himself. 'The boy looks very like her.'

A few days passed. Oliver was well enough to get up and Mr Brownlow bought him some new clothes.

The house in Pentonville was quiet and comfortable. Mr Brownlow and his housekeeper were very kind to Oliver.

Mr Brownlow did not ask Oliver many questions. He liked the young boy and thought he was honest. Oliver was happy for the first time in his life.

'You are very kind,' Oliver said one afternoon. 'Can I do something for you?'

'That's strange,' Mr Brownlow said. 'The boy looks
very like her.'

'Perhaps you can,' Mr Brownlow answered, with a smile. 'I have some books to return to the bookstall. And some money for the owner, too.'

'I'll take them for you, sir,' Oliver cried. 'Please let me. I am stronger now. Tell me the way. I'll run straight there and back!'

So Mr Brownlow gave Oliver the books and a five pound banknote.

The old gentleman and his housekeeper stood at the door and watched the boy run down the street. At the corner, Oliver turned and waved to them.

Mr Brownlow waved back. Then he looked at his watch.

'The boy will be back in twenty minutes,' he said.

———

Oliver was pleased that he was helping Mr Brownlow. The boy hurried along the streets with the books under his arm.

Suddenly, a young woman stepped out in front of him. She grabbed him by the arm.

'Oh, it's Oliver, my brother Oliver!' the girl cried. 'Come back to your sister and your parents!'

'Oh, it's Nancy!' Oliver cried in fear.

'That's right. Your dear sister, Nancy,' the girl said, holding Oliver tightly.

'No, no, I'm an orphan!' Oliver cried. 'I live with Mr Brownlow!'

Several people stopped to listen. They watched Nancy pull Oliver along the street. Bill Sikes now walked up with his dog.

'Oliver, you young villain[24], come back to your mother,' Bill said.

'No, no! Help me, someone!' Oliver screamed.

'Help you[25]? I'll help you!' Sikes shouted. 'What are these?' He grabbed the books from Oliver. 'Books! Stolen them, have you?

'Here's my help for you!' he shouted, hitting Oliver on the

head. 'Come, Bulls-eye!' Bill called to his dog. 'Stand next to him. Don't let him go!'

It was getting dark now. Sikes dragged[26] Oliver roughly along the narrow streets. The dog followed, growling[27] loudly.

In a short time, Oliver was back with Fagin. Fagin was delighted.

'I'm pleased to see you again,' he said, with a wicked[28] smile. 'You're looking very well, Oliver, my dear.'

'And look at his clothes – all new!' Charley cried.

'We'll look after them for you, Oliver,' Fagin said. 'They're too good to wear here!'

The Dodger was quietly taking things out of Oliver's pockets. He whistled in surprise and held up the five pound banknote.

'What's that? Money? That's mine!' Sikes cried, grabbing the banknote.

'No, no, Bill, my dear. You have the books,' Fagin said quickly.

'If I don't get the money I'll take the boy back,' Sikes shouted. 'Don't forget, Nancy and me found the boy!'

Oliver began to cry. 'The money belongs to Mr Brownlow and the books too. Please, please, send them back. He'll think I've stolen them!'

'Yes, he will, won't he?' Fagin said, with a laugh. 'It couldn't be better, could it, Bill? He's a thief now. He's one of us. We've got the boy for life!'

When he heard this, Oliver gave a great shriek. He ran wildly to the door, but the boys pulled him back.

'You want to call for help, do you?' Fagin said quietly. He picked up a stick. 'We'll stop that, my dear.'

The old man hit Oliver hard. He raised his arm to hit him again. But Nancy ran forward and grabbed the stick. She broke it and threw it on the floor.

'Leave the boy alone, Fagin,' the girl cried. 'I got him back for you. Isn't that enough?'

Bill Sikes laughed.

'You're a strange friend for the boy, Nancy!' he said. 'You caught him and brought him back. Now you want to help him. Be quiet, or I'll set the dog on you[29] – and on the boy too.'

'Do what you like with me, Bill, but don't hurt Oliver,' Nancy replied.

She turned to Fagin. 'You made me a thief. Now you'll make the boy a thief too!' she screamed. And then she began to cry.

Fagin did not listen to her. 'Charley,' he said, 'take off Oliver's nice new clothes. Then put him to bed. He must be tired.'

Oliver, alone and terrified, was locked in another room. He could not escape. The poor unhappy boy cried himself to sleep.

Mr Brownlow looked at his watch. One hour passed and then two.

Darkness fell, but Oliver did not return.

5

The Robbery

When Oliver woke next morning, there were no sounds from the other room. He was alone in the house. He waited unhappily for Fagin to return.

In the evening, Fagin came back carrying a pair of strong shoes.

'Put these on, Oliver, my dear,' the old man said. 'You have some walking to do.'

'Where am I going?' Oliver asked.

'Bill has a little job for you. Nancy will take you there. But don't worry, she'll bring you back!'

It was evening when Nancy arrived.

'Must I go with you?' Oliver whispered.

'Yes, Oliver, dear. Come along,' the girl replied sadly.

Without looking at Fagin, Nancy took hold of Oliver's hand. Soon they were walking quickly through the dark, crowded streets. They reached a house in Bethnal Green.

'Be quiet and you won't be hurt,' Nancy said. 'Bill Sikes is a cruel man. He often beats me! I'll try to help you soon, but I can't help you now.'

Bill Sikes was waiting for them in the house.

'Did the boy come quietly?' he asked.

'Very quietly,' Nancy answered.

'I'm pleased to hear it,' Sikes replied. 'Come here, boy. I've got something to show you.'

The man picked up a gun. 'You know what this is, don't you?' Sikes asked.

Oliver nodded his head.

'Yes, it's a gun and it's loaded,' Sikes went on.

He pointed the gun at the boy's head.

'If you speak one word when we're out – I'll shoot you,' Sikes said. 'Do you understand?'

'Yes, sir,' Oliver replied, shaking with fear.

'Right, then. Now, Nancy, my girl, bring us our supper. The boy and I must get up early tomorrow morning.'

———

It was still dark when Sikes woke Oliver.

'Be quick. Eat your breakfast. It's half past five,' Bill told the boy. Then he turned to Nancy.

'Don't leave the house. Stay here with the dog,' Sikes said.

The wind was blowing and it was raining hard. They walked all day. By the evening, London was left far behind and they had arrived at Shepperton. Oliver was exhausted.

They came to an old house with fields all around it. Sikes opened the door quietly.

'Who's that?' a rough voice cried.

'Toby, it's me,' Sikes answered, 'and one of Fagin's boys. The one I told you about. Give us something to eat, Toby. We've come a long way.'

Oliver was too tired to eat and soon he was fast asleep.

Toby woke Oliver at half past one the next morning. It was time to go. The two men wore long coats with the collars turned up. They wrapped scarves round their faces. Both men carried guns and lanterns[30].

Sikes held Oliver's hand. 'Take the boy's other hand, Toby,' he said.

It was very dark. There was a thick mist all around them as they walked over a bridge across a river. Soon they were walking along the streets of the small town of Chertsey. Everything was very quiet.

They reached a narrow road with fields on both sides. After a time, they came to an old house with a high wall round it.

Toby quickly climbed over the wall. He pulled Oliver over with him. Bill Sikes followed.

The two men led Oliver towards the house.

At last Oliver understood what was going to happen. The two men were going to break into the house. This was a robbery!

'For God's sake, let me go!' Oliver cried. 'Please, please, do not make me steal. Let me go! I won't tell anyone!'

'Quiet!' Sikes said roughly.

They were standing below a very small window. Toby climbed up and broke the lock and the window opened.

'Now listen,' Sikes whispered to Oliver, 'you're going through that window. Then I'll pass you a lantern.

'Go along the passage to the front door,' he went on. 'Open the door and let us in.'

Toby bent over. Sikes climbed onto his back. Then he dragged Oliver up with him. Sikes pushed Oliver through the window and gave him the lantern.

'Now go on,' the robber whispered. 'My gun is pointing at your back. Quiet now – and hurry!'

Oliver began to walk along the passage. He decided to cry out and wake the people in the house. Suddenly a dog barked and there was a shout from inside the house.

'Come back!' Sikes cried. 'They've heard us. Come back!'

Terrified, Oliver dropped the lantern. There was a crash and then another shout. The boy saw a light and two people at the top of the stairs. There was a loud bang. Oliver fell back towards the window.

'He's been shot!' Bill cried. 'We can't leave him here. He knows too much about us!'

The wounded boy was pulled back through the window. The two robbers carried him as they ran away. Oliver felt sick and very cold. Then he fainted.

Hours later, Oliver opened his eyes. It was daylight. He was lying by the side of the road. One arm was wet with blood. The pain was very bad. Oliver knew he would die if he stayed by the road. He began to walk slowly along the road. He came to a house with a high wall. He knew that this was the house that Bill and Toby had broken into. But he had to get help or he would die. He opened the gate and started to walk towards the door. Exhausted, he knocked on the door and fell to the ground. When Oliver opened his eyes again, two women were looking down at him.

'The poor child!' the older woman cried. 'Look, Rose, he is badly hurt. This was the boy with the robbers!'

When Oliver opened his eyes again, two women were looking down at him.

'And they left him to die,' the young woman said softly. 'Poor child, there is no wickedness in his sweet face. Aunt, we will look after him. We must put him to bed.'

'And get a doctor,' the older woman added.

So when Oliver woke again, he was in a soft white bed. His wounded arm was bandaged. He felt cool and clean.

The young woman's name was Rose Maylie. Later, Oliver told her his terrible story.

'You can stay here with us,' she said. 'Those evil men will never find you here.'

The young boy had found good friends. Oliver's terrible life in London was far away.

6

Monks

After they left Oliver, Toby and Sikes went in different directions. Toby went back to Fagin's house.

'Where's the boy?' Fagin cried. 'Where's the boy? Has Bill got him?'

'No,' Toby said. 'The boy was shot. We had to leave him.'

Fagin was mad with anger and fear.

'Was the boy alive or dead?' he cried.

'I don't know,' Toby replied.

'Don't know? You fool! That boy is very valuable to me!' the old man screamed.

'What about us?' Toby shouted. 'We nearly got caught last night. If the police catch us they'll hang us. We didn't want to be hanged because of a boy so we left him. I don't know if he's alive or dead.'

Fagin gave another cry of anger. Then he ran out of the house. He hurried along the dirty streets to Sikes' house. The anger on the old man's face was terrible. People turned away from him in fear.

Bill Sikes was not at home. His white dog growled at Fagin from a corner of the room. Nancy was sitting at the table. She had a glass and a bottle of gin in front of her.

'Where is Bill, my dear?' Fagin asked. 'Have you seen him?'

The girl shook her head and began to cry.

'I've seen Toby,' the old man went on. 'Poor little Oliver was hurt. Think of that, Nancy!'

'Oliver hurt? Where is he?' Nancy cried.

'They left him to die, Nancy, left him to die,' Fagin said softly.

'I hope he is dead!' Nancy shrieked. 'If he's dead, he's free. He's escaped from Bill and from you. I wish I was free. I hate all of you! Why did I bring him back from Pentonville?'

'You're drunk,' Fagin said. 'I don't care about Bill. He'll be hanged if he's caught. But I want that boy – alive.'

'And I hope he's dead,' the girl repeated. 'Now leave me alone, you old villain!'

Fagin did not answer. He left the girl and hurried home through the dark streets. He was outside his own door when someone called his name. The old man turned quickly.

'Is that you, Bill?' he whispered.

'No, it's Monks,' the voice replied.

A tall man stepped out of the shadow[31] of a dark doorway. He was dark-haired and young, but his face was thin and wrinkled. His dark eyes were as evil as Fagin's.

'Where have you been?' Monks asked in his hard voice.

'Working for you, my dear,' Fagin answered. 'Come upstairs.'

'Is anyone here?' Monks asked quickly.

'Only Toby and the boys,' Fagin said. 'And they're asleep. Come.'

Fagin lit a candle and the two men walked up the stairs to the top of the house.

'I'll leave the candle outside the door,' Fagin whispered. 'There are no curtains at the windows in this room. We must be careful. We don't want people in the street to see us.'

Fagin told Monks about the robbery at the house in Chertsey.

'It was badly planned[32],' Monks said. 'I came to you because I wanted the boy to be a thief. I want Oliver Twist to be caught by the police. I want him to go to prison.

'I am paying you to make him a thief,' Monks went on. 'I don't want him killed. Why did you send him with Sikes to rob that house? He wasn't ready.'

'Perhaps he wasn't,' Fagin said. 'But the boy can't steal from people's pockets. He went with the Dodger to steal handkerchiefs and he was caught. But he didn't go to prison. Oliver looks young and honest. Everyone believed he was a good, honest child.

'I'll get the boy back from Chertsey,' Fagin went on. 'I'll make him a thief – if he hasn't died already!'

'Died? I've told you before. I don't want him dead. I don't want to be blamed[33] for his death,' Monks said with a look of terror. He stopped suddenly.

'What's that?' he cried. 'I saw a shadow. The shape of a woman. Who is it?'

The old man ran out of the room and picked up the candle. He held the light above his head and looked down the stairs.

'There's no one here,' he said. 'You're afraid of shadows. You'd better go now. I'll let you know when I have news of the boy.'

Some weeks later, Oliver was sitting in his quiet room in the Maylies' house.

The air was still and it was very warm. There was a book in the boy's hands, but he was not reading it. He was nearly asleep.

Hearing a noise, Oliver looked up.

Two terrible faces were looking through the window. One was a thin, wrinkled face with dark, evil eyes. The other was the face of Fagin!

Oliver closed his eyes in horror. When he opened them, the two men had gone.

At first, Oliver was too terrified to move. Then he got up and looked out of the window. There was nobody there.

'It was a dream,' Oliver said to himself.

He did not tell Rose or her aunt, Mrs Maylie, what he had seen.

7

The Locket

Mr Bumble sighed loudly. He was not the parish beadle now. He did not have a fine hat and coat and a long stick to carry. Mr Bumble had a different job and it was a much more important one. He was the new master of the workhouse. But he was very unhappy.

Mr Bumble was unhappy because he was married. He had married the matron of the workhouse, Mrs Corney. Mrs Corney was now called Mrs Bumble. She was a hard, bad-tempered woman.

Suddenly Mrs Bumble hurried into the room. She looked at her husband who was half asleep in his chair.

'Are you going to sit there all day?' Mrs Bumble asked.

'I shall sit here as long as I like, Mrs Bumble,' her husband said. 'Why didn't your first husband teach you to be polite?'

Mrs Bumble gave a loud scream. Then she sat down and began to cry.

Mr Bumble smiled. He stood up and put on his hat.

'You can cry, Mrs Bumble,' he said. 'Cry as much as you like. I don't care!'

'Then I'll make you care[34]!' Mrs Bumble cried.

She jumped up from her chair and ran at him. She knocked off Mr Bumble's hat. Then she began hitting him and pulling his hair.

'Get out!' Mrs Bumble shouted. 'I don't want you here.'

Mr Bumble slowly put on his hat again.

'Are you going?' Mrs Bumble cried.

'Certainly, my dear, certainly,' Mr Bumble answered. 'I don't want to stay here with you!'

Mr Bumble walked slowly up the road towards the inn.

'When I was the beadle, I was respected[35],' Mr Bumble said sadly to himself. 'Now, everyone laughs at me.'

He went into the inn and bought a drink.

There was one other man there – a stranger.

The stranger was a young man, with a thin, wrinkled face. His eyes were full of hate and anger.

The young man looked at Mr Bumble carefully. Then he spoke.

'I have seen you before,' he said. 'Aren't you the beadle of this parish?'

'I was the beadle,' Mr Bumble said sadly. 'Now I'm master of the workhouse and a married man.'

'I came here to find you,' the young man said. 'I want some information. I'll pay you.'

And he placed two gold coins on the table.

Mr Bumble took the money quickly. 'I'll help you if I can,' he said.

'Then think back nearly twelve years,' the young man said. 'It was winter. The time was midnight. The place – the parish workhouse.'

Mr Bumble listened carefully.

'A boy was born at that time,' the young man went on.

'Many boys were born in the workhouse,' Mr Bumble said, 'and many died.'

'This boy didn't die. Eleven years later, he ran away. His name was . . .'

'Oliver Twist!' Mr Bumble cried. 'He was a young villain. I always said he . . .'

'I don't want to hear about Oliver Twist,' the young man said sharply. 'I want to talk to the matron of the workhouse. The matron was with the boy's mother when she died. How can I find this woman?'

'I can help you,' Mr Bumble replied. 'The matron is now my wife.'

'I think she has something I want,' the young man went on.

He gave Mr Bumble a dirty piece of paper.

'Give your wife this note,' the stranger said. 'It tells her what I want. There's an address written in the note too. Meet me at that address tomorrow night at nine o'clock. I'll give you more money then.'

'But you haven't told me your name,' Mr Bumble said.

'Monks. My name is Monks,' the young man said.

The next night, as Mr and Mrs Bumble went to meet Monks, there was a terrible storm. They were soon wet through.

Monk's note had told them to go to an old building by a river. They found the old building and knocked on the door.

Monks opened the door at once. He looked at Mrs Bumble.

'I think you have something for me,' Monks said, with an evil smile. 'Come in.'

The Bumbles followed Monks into a dark little room. They sat down. Monks spoke first.

'Now madam, nearly twelve years ago, you stole a gold locket.'

'No, No! The girl gave me the locket. I was keeping it for the child. But he ran away. If you want the locket, give me £25.'

'Show me the locket first.'

Mrs Bumble put a small leather bag on the table.

'Now give me the money!' she said.

'Wait!' said Monks. He opened the bag and took out the gold locket. Monks opened it carefully and looked inside.

'Two pieces of hair and a gold wedding-ring,' he said.

'The name "Agnes" is written inside the ring,' Mrs Bumble said quickly. 'And a date. The child was born less than a year after that date.'

'Good,' Monks said. He walked to the window and opened it. Below the window was the river.

Monks put a stone in the bag with the locket. Then he threw the bag into the middle of the river. Monks closed the window quickly.

'Here's your money,' the young man said. 'Forget this evening and forget me. If we meet again, I shall not know you. Now go quickly!'

8

Nancy's Plan

Oliver lived very happily with his new friends. Rose Maylie and her aunt were very kind to him. But his enemies had not forgotten him.

Bill Sikes had bad luck after the failed robbery at Chertsey. Toby and Sikes had not been able to steal anything from the house. And now Bill had become ill. He had caught a fever

Monks opened the locket carefully and looked inside.

and was very thin. He had no money and not enough to eat. He became more bad-tempered.

Nancy had become pale and thin. But she looked after Sikes with great care. She cooked his food and gave him medicine.

'How do you feel tonight, Bill?' Nancy asked.

'I'm very weak,' Sikes replied. 'Help me off this bed and onto a chair.'

Nancy was not strong enough to hold the heavy man, so he fell onto the chair.

Sikes hit her. 'If you can't help me,' he said, 'leave now. And don't start crying, or I'll hit you again.'

The girl was so exhausted that she fainted. Sikes shook her and began to shout.

At that moment, Fagin came into the room.

'Why are you here?' Sikes asked him angrily.

'To help you, of course, my dear,' the old man answered. 'Look what we've brought you, Bill.'

The Artful Dodger and Charley followed Fagin into the room. They were carrying baskets of food and drink.

'Dodger, my dear,' Fagin said, 'show Bill what you've got. And give Nancy a drink.'

'I've been ill for three weeks. Why didn't you come here earlier?' Bill asked. He began to eat and drink like an animal. As Bill drank, he became happier. He told Nancy to start eating too.

But Bill Sikes was still angry with Fagin.

'I need money,' said Sikes to the old man. 'And I need it tonight.'

Fagin sighed loudly.

'Well, I'll send the Dodger to you with a little money,' he said.

'No, don't give the money to the Dodger,' Sikes answered. 'I'll never get it. Nancy can go back with you. Give the money to her. I'm going to sleep.'

Fagin agreed.

'It's time you started work,' Fagin said to the Dodger and Charley. 'Off you go.' Then he walked slowly back to his house with Nancy.

When they reached the dark and dirty house, Fagin lit a candle.

'Wait here,' he said to Nancy. 'I'll go and get the money.'

The girl sat down at the table, put her head on her arms and closed her eyes.

There was a knock at the door downstairs. Fagin hurried down, carrying the candle.

As he opened the door, Fagin said in surprise, 'Monks!'

The young man came in quickly. But he stopped when he saw Nancy.

'Nancy works for me,' Fagin said, with a smile. 'Don't worry about her.

'When did you get back? Did you find the parish beadle?' Fagin went on.

'I got back two hours ago. I did find him and I've got good news,' Monks answered. 'We must talk. But not here.'

'We'll go upstairs,' Fagin said. He looked quickly at Nancy. Her head was on her arms and her eyes were shut. But Nancy was not asleep. As soon as the men left the room, Nancy followed them.

A quarter of an hour later, Nancy returned. She sat down at the table.

She heard Monks leave the house. Then Fagin came into the room again.

'Here's the money for Bill,' he said.

'You've taken a long time, Fagin,' Nancy said.

The old man stared at the girl. Then he gave her the coins.

'You look very pale, my dear,' Fagin said. 'What's the matter?'

'Nancy works for me,' Fagin said, with a smile.
'Don't worry about her.'

'I'm very tired,' Nancy answered quickly. 'I must go back to Bethnal Green now. Bill gets angry if I'm away too long.'

But when Nancy was in the street, she stopped for a moment. Then she began to walk quickly. She did not walk towards Bill Sikes' house in Bethnal Green.

The terrified girl walked faster and faster. Soon she was running through the crowded streets.

Suddenly she stopped. She was pale and shaking with fear. Then she turned and ran back, towards Sikes' house.

When she got to the house, the robber was drinking gin. He took the money from the girl and went on drinking. Nancy stayed with him. But as time passed, she began to walk about the room. The girl's face was white and her eyes were very bright. Sikes glared at her. Then he spoke.

'What's the matter with you?' Sikes asked. 'Are you ill? Have you caught a fever? Or are you planning to do something?'

Nancy did not reply. She continued to walk about nervously.

Then Sikes said in a loud voice, 'Give me my medicine. Then sit by me. I'm going to sleep.'

Nancy carefully filled a glass with medicine. Then she held the glass to Bill's lips until he had drunk it all.

Bill's eyes closed, opened and then closed again. Sikes was asleep. The medicine was a powerful drug and Nancy had given the robber all of it.

'Thank God. He'll sleep for many hours now,' Nancy whispered. Then she kissed Bill gently and left the room.

It was night, but the narrow streets were crowded with people. Nancy soon reached a part of the city where rich people lived. Here the streets were nearly empty. Nancy began to run.

At last she stopped outside a quiet hotel near Hyde Park. She went inside.

The hotel porter looked up from his desk and spoke to the girl.

'Now then, what are you doing here?' he said. He spoke sharply to the poorly-dressed girl.

'I want to see a lady. She's staying here,' Nancy said.

'What lady?' the porter asked.

'Miss Rose Maylie,' Nancy replied.

'Miss Maylie has nothing to say to you,' the porter said. 'We don't want you here. Go away!'

At that moment, a young woman came down the stairs. Nancy ran up to her.

'Oh, please, please help me!' she cried. 'I must see Miss Maylie!'

'I am Miss Maylie,' the young woman said quietly. 'Why do you wish to see me?'

At Rose's kind words, Nancy started to cry. Rose Maylie took the girl to her bedroom in the hotel.

'Oh, lady,' Nancy said, 'I am the wicked girl who took Oliver Twist back to his enemies!'

'You?' Rose cried.

'Yes. And I am very sorry,' Nancy went on. 'I am in great danger. If Oliver's enemies knew I was here, they would kill me. Do you know a man called Monks?'

'Monks? No. Who is he?' Rose asked.

'Someone who wishes to harm[36] Oliver,' Nancy replied. 'Monks knows a wicked old man, called Fagin.

'I heard them talking together,' Nancy went on. 'Monks is Oliver's brother!'

'His brother?' Rose repeated in surprise.

'Yes, but Monks hates the child. Monks knows everything about Oliver – where he was born and how he came to London. Monks knows all about you. He knows that Oliver is living with you and your aunt. He knows that you are staying at this hotel. Monks wants to harm Oliver.

'I have lived with evil men all my life. But Monks is one of the most evil men I have ever known.'

'What can I do?' Rose cried. She thought for a moment and then spoke again.

'Stay here with me,' she said to Nancy. 'You will be safe here. I will find someone to help us.'

'Lady, I cannot stay any longer. I must go back,' Nancy answered. 'My friends are bad. But I must go back to them. It is too late to change my life now.

'We must try to help Oliver,' Nancy went on. 'His enemies plan to take him from you and make him a thief.'

'You must tell me more. Where can I find you again?' asked Rose.

'Every Saturday night,' said Nancy, 'between eleven and twelve, I will walk on London Bridge – if I am alive.

'Meet me there. Bring a friend who can help us. I must go now. I cannot stay any longer. Goodbye and thank you.'

And, without saying another word, Nancy was gone.

9

On London Bridge

Oliver was with Rose in London. Oliver had told Rose all about his life in London. He had told her about Mr Brownlow and how Mr Brownlow had been kind to him. Rose had brought Oliver to London to find Mr Brownlow. Every day Oliver was taken round the streets of London in Rose's carriage. Oliver thought he might see Mr Brownlow or Mr Brownlow's house.

The morning after Nancy's visit, Oliver ran into Rose's room.

'I have seen him! I have seen Mr Brownlow!' Oliver cried. 'I saw him going into his house.'

'Thank God,' Rose said. 'I am pleased we have found him. And he can help us now. I shall visit him at once.'

Rose went to Pentonville to visit the kind old gentleman.

'You don't know me,' Rose began, 'but you once showed kindness to a young friend of mine – Oliver Twist.'

'Oliver Twist!' Mr Brownlow repeated. 'Where is the poor boy? Is he safe?'

Then Rose told Mr Brownlow Oliver's story. She told him of her meeting with Nancy at the hotel.

'Where is the child now?' Mr Brownlow asked.

'He is in my carriage,' Rose said. 'He wants to see you.'

Mr Brownlow hurried outside to the carriage. He spoke to Oliver with the greatest kindness. Mr Brownlow's housekeeper heard that Oliver had returned. She was delighted to see the boy.

'I knew the dear child would come back, I knew it!' she cried.

Mr Brownlow took Rose into the library.

'We must be very careful,' the old gentleman said. 'Fagin and Monks are very wicked men. We must find Monks and make him tell us everything. Perhaps Nancy can help us. I will walk with you on London Bridge next Sunday evening.

'Until Sunday, you and Oliver must stay with me.'

'Thank you,' Rose said with a smile.

―――――

Sunday night came. A clock struck eleven. Nancy, Fagin and Sikes were in Bill's house in Bethnal Green. Nancy was now desperate with fear. Nancy got up from her chair and put on her hat. Fagin and Sikes looked at her in surprise.

'What are you doing, girl?' Sikes asked. 'Where are you going at this time of night?'

'I don't know. I'm ill. I need to go outside and breathe the air,' the girl replied quickly.

'Then put your head out of the window and breathe the air!' Sikes told her, with a laugh. 'You're not going out!'

He went to the door, locked it and put the key in his pocket. Nancy began to cry loudly.

'Let me go out, Bill, just for an hour!' she screamed. 'Fagin, tell Bill to let me go out!'

'Stop that noise, or I'll set the dog on you!' Sikes cried.

'Never, never! Let me go! Let me go!'

Sikes pushed Nancy down into a chair. She fought and cried for a long time. Then the clock struck twelve. Immediately she became quiet.

'Something's wrong with the girl,' said Sikes.

'You're right, Bill. Keep her in the house,' Fagin said slowly. 'I must go home now.'

Fagin thought carefully as he hurried through the dark streets. Why was Nancy behaving[37] so strangely?

'Perhaps Nancy doesn't love Bill any more,' Fagin said to himself. 'If Bill finds out, he'll kill Nancy. Sikes is a dangerous man. I don't need him any more. If Nancy hates Bill, perhaps I can get her to kill him!'

Fagin laughed. 'I'll find out why she's behaving so strangely. I'll find out her secret,' the old man said.

———

A week had passed. It was a quarter to midnight on Sunday. Two people were on London Bridge. One of them was Nancy. She was walking up and down nervously. The other person was a boy. He was hiding in the shadows.

A carriage stopped on the bridge. A young woman and a man got out. Nancy ran towards them.

'Thank God you've come,' Nancy said. 'But there's too much light here. Someone will see us. Come to the other end of the bridge. There are some steps down to the river. We can talk in the darkness.'

'Are you afraid of the light?' Mr Brownlow asked quietly.

'I am afraid of everything tonight,' Nancy answered. 'I think I am going to die soon.'

'The poor girl!' Rose whispered, as they followed Nancy to the other end of the bridge. On the dark steps by the water, Rose spoke again.

'What can you tell us?' she asked.

'I know where you can find Monks,' Nancy replied.

'Good. Tell us quickly,' Mr Brownlow said.

Nancy told them all she knew about Monks and Fagin's plans.

'What does Monks look like?' Mr Brownlow asked.

'He is a tall man – about thirty years old,' Nancy replied. 'But he looks much older. His face is thin and wrinkled and his eyes are dark and cruel.'

'I'll find him,' said Mr Brownlow. 'But how can we help you?'

'You cannot help me,' Nancy answered.

'What do you mean?' Mr Brownlow asked kindly. 'You must leave these evil men. We will find them and tell the police. They will go to prison. But you will be safe.'

'No, no,' Nancy whispered. 'I cannot help you catch them.'

'We can help you escape from them. You can leave the country. You can start a new life,' replied Mr Brownlow.

'I hate my life, but I cannot change it now,' Nancy answered slowly. 'I must go home.

'Goodnight, sir, and goodnight to you, sweet lady,' Nancy added. 'I don't think we shall meet again. Leave me now – please.'

Mr Brownlow and Rose walked sadly back across the bridge. Nancy waited on the steps. She heard the carriage drive away. Then she walked quickly back to the poor street where she lived.

Behind her, in the shadows, a boy followed.

Nancy told them all she knew about Monks and Fagin's plans.

10

Murder!

It was four o'clock in the morning. Fagin was sitting alone. His evil face was twisted with fear and hatred.

There was a loud knock at the front door.

'That's Bill. At last!' Fagin whispered.

Fagin went downstairs and unlocked the door. Sikes pushed past him. He had a heavy bundle[38] under his arm. He threw the bundle on the table.

'Here's some things for you to sell. They're worth a lot. So pay me well,' Sikes said. 'Now get me a drink, you old villain!'

Then Sikes saw that Fagin was angry.

'What's happened?' he said. 'Tell me quickly. I've got to get back to Nancy. She'll think I've been caught by the police.'

'Caught? Yes, you soon will be caught!' Fagin replied in a terrible voice. 'Someone's been talking about us. Someone wants to get us hanged.'

'Who is he?' Sikes shouted. 'Tell me his name and I'll smash his head in!'

'Not *he*, Bill, *she*,' Fagin said softly.

'Hell's fire[39]!' Sikes cried. 'Are you talking about . . .?'

'Yes – Nancy!' Fagin replied, with a wicked smile.

'Nancy! But how do you know?' Sikes shouted.

Fagin went into the next room. The old man shook the Dodger awake. Then he dragged him towards Sikes.

'Tell Bill what you heard, Dodger,' Fagin said. 'Tell him – or I'll kill you!'

Sikes listened to the boy's story. He gave a great shout of anger.

'Let me get her!' Sikes cried. 'I'll . . .'

'Wait a minute, Bill,' Fagin said, standing in front of the door.

'Don't be too violent[40], Bill,' the old man said quietly.

'I mean, we must be careful,' Fagin added slowly. 'Don't be too violent, Bill. Go and find Nancy. But be careful. No one must find out what you do.'

Without speaking, Sikes pushed past Fagin and ran out of the house.

When he reached home, Sikes went up the stairs quietly. He locked the door behind him. Nancy was asleep on the bed. Bill's white dog, Bulls-eye, was lying underneath a table in the corner of the room.

Bill shook Nancy roughly. 'Get up!' he said.

Nancy opened her eyes and smiled. 'Hello Bill, you're home,' she said.

Nancy got up and went to the window.

'Don't open the curtains,' Sikes said. 'There's enough light in the room.'

'Why are you looking at me like that, Bill?' Nancy cried. 'What's wrong?'

Sikes glared at Nancy for a few moments. Then he took hold of her hair. He pulled her away from the window.

Nancy cried out in pain. 'Bill, please! Tell me what I've done!'

'You know, you devil,' Sikes replied. 'You were followed last night. Someone was listening to every word you said!'

Nancy gave a terrible cry.

'I didn't say anything about you, Bill, I didn't!' the girl shrieked. 'I said nothing about you. I only spoke about Monks. If you kill me, they'll hang you. Let me go and you can escape before the police catch Fagin and Monks.'

Sikes did not reply, but took his gun out of his pocket. He did not fire it, but, with all his strength, Sikes hit the girl twice across her face.

Nancy cried out and fell to the ground. Blood was pouring from her head. She tried to stand up.

*Nancy cried out in pain. 'Bill, please! Tell me
what I've done!'*

Sikes was mad with anger. He picked up a thick stick and hit her again and again. The poor girl was dead.

Hours passed. Sunlight shone into the room.

The girl's body lay on the floor, covered with blood. Her eyes were open. There was blood on the floor, blood on Sikes' clothes. Sikes lit a fire and burnt the heavy stick. He washed himself carefully. He tried to wash the blood from his clothes. Sikes could not turn away from Nancy. Her dead eyes stared at him.

At last, dragging the dog after him, Sikes left the room. He locked the door.

Sikes stood in the street and looked up at the window. Then he whistled for the dog to follow him and walked quickly away.

It was dark now. Sikes walked on and on through the empty streets. He reached the edge of the city. There were no houses now, just fields. But he went on walking.

That night the murderer rested in a wood. But he could not sleep. He was terrified of every sound. The next day he walked on. But where was he going? Where could he hide?

'I'll go back to London,' Sikes said to himself. 'The police won't find me there. Fagin will hide me. I'll get money from Fagin and leave the country.'

So Sikes started to walk back towards London. The white dog followed him.

'The dog!' Sikes said to himself. 'If they find the dog, they'll find me. I'll drown[41] it.'

Sikes stopped by a pool of water. He picked up a big stone and tied it into his scarf[42].

'Come here,' Sikes said quietly to the dog. 'Bulls-eye, come here!'

The dog took a few steps forward. Then it stopped.

'Come here, Bulls eye!' Sikes shouted.

The dog growled and ran back a few steps.

'Come here!' Sikes shouted again.

The dog looked at him for a moment. Then, suddenly, it turned and ran away, as fast as it could.

Sikes whistled again and again. But the dog did not return.

Sikes began to walk back to London.

11

Oliver's Brother

A few days later, a carriage stopped outside Mr Brownlow's house. Mr Brownlow got out. Then two servants took a young man out of the carriage. They led him into the house.

'Now, young man,' said Mr Brownlow, 'you must tell me everything I want to know. If you try to leave, I shall call the police. You must decide what you want to do.'

'Is there no other way?' the young man asked.

'No,' Mr Brownlow said.

The young man followed Mr Brownlow into his library. Mr Brownlow looked at the young man for a few moments. Then he began to speak.

'You call yourself Monks. That is not your real name,' Mr Brownlow said. 'Your parents are dead. But you have a younger brother.'

'I have no brother,' Monks said quickly.

'Listen to me,' Mr Brownlow said. 'As a young man, your father was made to get married. The woman was ten years older than him. Their marriage was never happy. You were born. Some years later, your parents separated[43].'

'How do you know this?' Monks asked angrily.

'Your father was my closest friend,' Mr Brownlow replied.

51

'Go on,' Monks said.

'Your mother left the country, taking you with her. Then your father met a young girl called Agnes Fleming. They fell in love. Soon, she was expecting a child[44].'

Monks smiled but said nothing. Mr Brownlow went on speaking.

'Your father inherited[45] a lot of money,' he said. 'He left England and went to live abroad. There he fell ill and died. When he died no one could find his will. All your father's money went to you and your mother. Agnes Fleming did not get anything.'

'And that cannot be changed,' Monks said.

'You are wrong,' Mr Brownlow replied. 'I know that your father made a will. You have read it. But you and your mother destroyed[46] it.'

'Why do you believe this?' Monks asked, with a cruel smile.

'Listen to me,' Mr Brownlow said. 'Before he went abroad, your father came to me. He said that he had separated from your mother. He gave me a picture of Agnes Fleming, the girl he loved. He told me about his love for Agnes. The portrait is on the wall behind you.'

Monks turned. He looked at the picture in horror.

'I see that you are surprised,' said Mr Brownlow. 'When I saw Oliver Twist beside the portrait, I knew that he was her son. You know this too.'

Monks said nothing. Mr Brownlow went on speaking.

'Your father told me that he had made a new will. Half of his money was to go to Agnes and her child. The rest of the money was for you and your mother.

'I never saw your father again,' Mr Brownlow went on sadly. 'I tried to find Agnes Fleming, but I could not. Many years later, you found her child. You tried to destroy the boy by making him a thief. You were afraid to kill him. But now there has been a murder.'

'A murder!' Monks repeated in horror.

'Yes, the murder of a poor girl who tried to help Oliver. Your evil friends will hang because they murdered her. You should be hanged too!'

Monks walked up and down the room. His dark eyes were full of fear.

'I have written all this down,' Mr Brownlow said. 'You must sign the paper. Oliver must have half of his father's money. Then you must leave the country. Do you agree?'

'I agree. I have no choice,' Monks said.

12

The Murderers Die

The robber, Toby, was hiding in an old house by the river in Bermondsey. He was staring at an exhausted white dog.

'Why has Bill's dog come here?' Toby asked himself. 'Is Bill coming here? Does the dog know this?'

Toby gave Bulls-eye some water. Then the robber sat waiting quietly.

There was a loud knock at the door. The dog began to howl[47].

Toby took a candle and went downstairs. A minute later, he returned to the room with Sikes.

The murderer untied the scarf from his face. Sikes was very pale. He was shaking with fear. He picked up a chair, pushed it against the wall and sat down.

'So the dog's here,' Sikes said roughly.

Toby said nothing.

'Somebody said the police have got Fagin. Is that true?' Sikes asked.

'Yes. They took him this afternoon. At about two o'clock,' Toby replied.

'Me and Charley got away. But they caught Fagin and the Dodger. And the Dodger has turned King's evidence[48].'

'Then Fagin will be hanged,' Sikes whispered.

Toby did not answer.

'Hell's fire!' Sikes cried out. 'Have you nothing to say to me? Are you going to tell the police about me – or help me?'

'You can stay here,' Toby answered slowly. There was another knock at the door. Toby went downstairs quickly. He returned with Charley Bates.

When the boy saw Sikes, he was horrified.

'Charley,' Sikes said, standing up, 'don't you remember your friend, Bill?'

'Don't come near me!' Charley cried. 'I know what you did. But I'm not afraid of you – you murderer! I'm going to see you hanged.'

And the boy began to shout loudly. 'Murder! Help! Murder! Murder!'

Sikes grabbed the boy. But Charley went on shouting.

There was a noise outside the house. Toby ran to the window and looked down. There were lights and the sound of footsteps coming nearer.

'Help! Help!' shrieked the boy. 'He's here! The murderer's here! Break down the door!'

Sikes dragged the boy upstairs into a room near the top of the house. He locked the door, then went back downstairs.

'Is the front door locked?' he asked Toby.

'Yes, it is,' Toby replied.

Sikes ran to the window and looked down to the street below.

'You won't get me!' he shouted to the people below. 'You won't catch Bill Sikes!'

The crowd shouted at him. Some people wanted to burn the house down. Some people wanted to climb up and catch him.

Sikes moved away from the window.

'I'm going to jump into the ditch behind the house,' Sikes said.

He picked up some rope, ran upstairs and out onto the roof.

Charley looked through a window and watched Sikes climb onto the steep roof. He began to shout to the crowd of people again.

'Go to the back of the house! Sikes is on the roof!' the boy cried.

Sikes ran across the roof of the house and looked down at the ditch. The ditch carried water from the river.

There was not much water in the ditch. And the soft mud was deep.

There was a crowd of people at the back of the house now. They were carrying lanterns. Sikes saw the angry faces staring up at him.

Sikes looked up. The houses on the other side of the ditch were full of people. There were people looking at him from every window.

Sikes tied one end of the rope to the chimneys. He made a noose[49] at the other end of the rope. He was going to put this round his body and climb down to the ditch.

Sikes put the noose over his head. He was going to pull the noose down, under his arms, but suddenly he turned round.

'Her eyes! I can see her eyes!' Sikes cried.

He stepped back and fell off the roof. The noose was round his neck. As he fell, the noose pulled tight. And the murderer hung there – dead!

Bulls-eye had followed Sikes onto the roof. With a howl, the dog tried to jump onto the dead man's shoulders. But the dog fell from the roof and it died in the ditch below.

———

Fagin was alone in the condemned cells[50]. It was Sunday. Fagin's last day.

Sikes tied one end of the rope to the chimneys. He made a noose at the other end of the rope.

As the hours passed, the old man shrieked and tore his hair with his hands.

Fagin walked round and round his small cell. He howled like an animal. But still the hours passed. Night came, but he could not sleep.

The clock struck eleven. At eight o'clock tomorrow morning, he would die.

Fagin thought of the murder of Nancy. He thought of the death of Bill Sikes.

Twelve o'clock struck, then one, two, three, four, five, six, seven, eight!

The cell door opened. Fagin was led out to be hanged. A great cry went up from the waiting crowd.

There was silence. Then there was another cry – a shout of joy.

Fagin was dead.

Epilogue

Monks left England and went to America. He died in prison. Mr Brownlow bought a house in Chertsey near the Maylies' house. He took Oliver into his home and Oliver became his son.

Points for Understanding

Prologue

1 What happens to the baby's mother? What is going to happen to the baby?
2 What does Mrs Corney take from the mother?

1

1 Why did Oliver ask the master of the workhouse for more gruel?
2 What does Mr Bumble do with Oliver?
3 Oliver decides to run away to London. Who does he meet? How does this person help Oliver?

2

1 Oliver meets a man. What is the man called? What does he look like?
2 The man and the boys play a game. Describe the game.
3 'You'll be as good as the Dodger one day!' What do the man's words mean? Does Oliver understand these words?

3

1 What does Oliver do while the the boys are out every morning?
2 'That boy's got my handkerchief!' What has happened? What does Oliver do? Who shouts 'Stop thief! Stop thief!'
3 Two men help Oliver. Who are they? What do they do and say?
4 Why is Fagin angry with Charley and the Dodger?
5 'Nancy, my dear, you can go,' Fagin says. What does he want her to do?

4

1 'The boy looks very like her.' Who is Mr Brownlow talking about?
2 What does Oliver do to help Mr Brownlow?
3 Oliver is pulled roughly along the narrow streets. What happens next?
4 'He's a thief now. He's one of us.' What does Fagin mean?

5

1 Where does Nancy take Oliver?
2 Where does Sikes take Oliver? Who do they meet?
3 Why do they go to a house in Chertsey? What happens in the house?
4 Where is Oliver when he opens his eyes a few hours later? Where does he go?

6

1 What does Fagin ask Toby? What does Toby reply?
2 What does Fagin tell Nancy when he goes to Bill Sikes' house?
3 Who does Fagin meet outside his house? Describe this person.
4 This person has paid Fagin to do something. What has he paid him to do?
5 Why did Fagin send Oliver to do the robbery at Chertsey?

7

1 Mr Bumble goes to the inn. Who does he meet?
2 Mr and Mrs Bumble meet the stranger. Where do they meet him?
3 What is in the leather bag? What does the stranger do with the bag?

8

1 Bill asks Fagin for money. What does Fagin say he will do? What does Bill want Fagin to do?
2 Nancy and Fagin go to Fagin's house. Who comes to visit Fagin? Where does Fagin take this person? What does Nancy do now?
3 Nancy gives Bill some medicine. What does she do then?
4 What information does Nancy give Rose about Oliver and Monks?

9

1 Rose meets Mr Brownlow. What does Rose tell him?
2 Who is on London Bridge at a quarter to midnight on Sunday? Why?

10

1 What information does the Dodger give to Bill Sikes? What does Fagin say to Bill?
2 What does Bill do when he gets home? Does he follow Fagin's advice?
3 Sikes leaves his house in Bethnal Green. Where does he go?

11

1 What does Mr Brownlow know about Monks' father?
2 Monks' father died. What happened to his will? Who got his money?
3 Why is Monks horrified when he sees the portrait in the library?
4 Monks' father made a new will. Who was going to inherit his money?
5 Monks found Oliver, Agnes Fleming's child. What did Monks decide to do to Oliver Twist?
6 What three things does Mr Brownlow make Monks do?

12

1 Sikes meets Toby at a house by the river. What does Toby tell Sikes?
2 What does Charley Bates do when he sees Sikes?
3 Sikes decides to try to escape. What does he do? What goes wrong?
4 What is a condemned cell? What happens to Fagin?

Glossary

1 **sigh** (page 6)
a noise you make when you are sad or tired.
2 **matron** (page 6)
(see A Note About England in the Nineteenth Century – page 5)
3 **parish workhouse** (page 6)
(see A Note About England in the Nineteenth Century – page 5)
4 **orphan** (page 6)
someone whose mother and father have died.
5 **no name and no wedding ring** (page 6)
the doctor means that the young mother has not told them her name and she has no wedding-ring on her finger. The young mother was not married to the child's father.
6 **locket** (page 6)
a piece of jewellery which is worn on a chain round the neck. Lockets can be opened. Inside you can keep small pictures of people you love, or pieces of their hair.
7 **beadle** (page 7)
(see A Note About England in the Nineteenth Century – page 5)

8 **gruel** (page 7)
a thin liquid meal made from oats (a kind of grain) and water.

9 **desperate** (page 7)
ready to do something difficult and dangerous. The boys in the workhouse were beaten and did not get enough to eat. They were so hungry that they had to get more food.

10 **shriek** (page 7)
a loud cry. Someone shrieks if they are angry or very frightened.

11 **glared** (page 8)
looked at someone angrily.

12 **hanged** (page 8)
(see *A Note About England in the Nineteenth Century* – page 5)

13 **apprentice** (page 8)
an apprentice was a young person who worked for somebody for a number of years and learnt how to do a job. An amount of money was paid to the person who taught an apprentice.

14 **begged** (page 8)
Oliver asked people for food because he had no money to buy any.

15 **whistled** (page 10)
to whistle is to make a noise through a small hole between your lips. You can whistle to make someone see you are there. You can whistle to show you are surprised. You can whistle to call a dog to you.

16 **wrinkled** (page 11)
covered in lines. Skin becomes wrinkled when people grow old.

17 **sack** (page 11)
a bag made of strong, rough cloth.

18 **silk handkerchief** (page 11)
a square piece of cloth you use to wipe your nose. Rich people had handkerchiefs made of silk – thin, soft cloth.

19 **grabbed** (page 12)
took hold of very quickly and roughly.

20 **wallet** (page 12)
a small leather container in which banknotes are kept.

21 **square** (page 15)
an open space in a town with buildings round it on four sides.

22 **call a cab** (page 16)
a cab is a carriage pulled by a horse. You pay the driver to take you where you want to go. There were many cabs in London at this time. Mr Brownlow asks someone to get a cab to come to him.

23 **housekeeper** (page 20)
a woman paid by Mr Brownlow to look after his house.
24 **villain** (page 22)
an evil person.
25 **help you** (page 22)
Bill Sikes is making a cruel joke. He is not going to help Oliver –
he is going to hurt him.
26 **dragged** (page 23)
pulled along roughly. You drag someone who does not want to go
with you.
27 **growling** (page 23)
making a loud, angry noise. Angry or frightened dogs growl.
28 **wicked** (page 23)
very, very bad; evil.
29 **set the dog on you** (page 24)
if someone sets a dog on you, they tell the dog to attack you.
30 **lantern** (page 26)
a metal container with a candle inside, which gives light.
31 **shadow** (page 30)
a dark place that light cannot reach. A shadow is also a dark
shape that is made when a person or a thing is in front of a light.
32 **badly planned** (page 31)
not thought about carefully. If you plan something, you decide
carefully what you are going to do.
33 **blamed** (page 31)
if you are blamed for something, people say you did something
wrong.
34 **I'll make you care** (page 33)
Mr Bumble has said he doesn't care if Mrs Bumble is upset. Mrs
Bumble is replying that she is going to hurt Mr Bumble because
he has said this.
35 **respected** (page 33)
if you are respected, people think you are a good person.
36 **harm** (page 41)
want to hurt someone and make their life unhappy.
37 **behaving** (page 44)
doing things in a special way. Fagin has seen that Nancy is doing
and saying things in a strange way.
38 **bundle** (page 47)
things held together in a piece of cloth.

39 **Hell's fire** (page 47)
Bill is saying these words because he is very angry.
40 **violent** (page 48)
if you are violent you hurt somebody very badly.
41 **drown** (page 50)
to drown is to die in water because you cannot breathe.
42 **scarf** (page 50)
a long piece of cloth worn round the neck.
43 **separated** (page 51)
if a husband and wife separate, they decide not to live with each other.
44 **expecting a child** (page 52)
going to have a baby.
45 **inherited** (page 52)
if you inherit money, you get it from a person who has died. A person writes a piece of paper called a will before they die. In the will they write the names of the people who are going to inherit their money. If there is no will, a person's money goes to their family. This is why Monks and his mother got money from Oliver's father, and Agnes Fleming got nothing.
46 **destroyed** (page 52)
damage something very badly so it cannot be used any more.
47 **howl** (page 53)
if a dog howls it makes a noise because it is upset or in pain.
48 **the Dodger has turned King's evidence** (page 54)
the Dodger is a criminal who has been caught. But he has told the police and the court all about crimes that other people, like Fagin, have done. He has given evidence against them. He has given this evidence so he will not be punished as much as they will. They will be hanged and he will just go to prison. The police and the courts are doing their work for the King and for England, so it is said that the Dodger had turned King's evidence.
49 **noose** (page 55)
a piece of rope that is tied into a circle. A noose in a rope can be pulled tight round something.
50 **condemned cell** (page 55)
a special room in a prison. Criminals were killed if they had murdered someone or stolen something. They were condemned to death. They were killed by being hanged with a rope round their necks. Prisoners who were going to be hanged were put in a condemned cell.

63

Exercises

Multiple Choice 1

Tick the best answer.

1 What were *workhouses*?
a ☐ They were factories that employed many working people.
b ☐ They were hostels where working men could rent rooms cheaply.
c ☐ They were places where working men could find jobs.
d ☑ They were places to house the poor, including orphans.

2 Who thought of the name *Oliver Twist* and why?
a ☐ Mrs Corney, because she liked to twist Oliver's ear.
b ☐ The workhouse master, because he thought it was Oliver's real name.
c ☐ Mr Bumble, because he gave names to boys in alphabetical order.
d ☐ The other boys, because they twisted Oliver's arm to ask for more food.

3 Why did Oliver have to leave the workhouse?
a ☐ He told Mrs Corney she was cruel.
b ☐ He asked for another bowl of gruel.
c ☐ He called Mr Bumble fat and stupid.
d ☐ He was old enough to go to work.

4 What did the beadle want to do with Oliver?
a ☐ Send him to join the navy.
b ☐ Send him to work in a coal mine.
c ☐ Sell him to a master as an apprentice.
d ☐ Make him walk all the way to London.

5 Why did Oliver run away from the workhouse?
a ☐ Because he wanted to go to London.
b ☐ Because he was afraid he would die if he stayed.
c ☐ Because he wanted to find his family.
d ☐ Because he was frightened of the other boys at the workhouse.

Oliver Goes to London

Complete the gaps. Use each word in the box once.

> boy   nowhere   eyes   help   work   nose   safe   for
> some   came   road   matter   know   tired   worry
> edge   gentleman   ~~days~~   began   name

Oliver walked for seven [1]........*days*........ . He wanted to find

[2]................................ in London, and he thought he would be

[3]........................... from Mr Bumble there. He begged [4]...........................

food. At last he [5].............................. to Barnet which is on the

[6].............................. of London. Here, he sat down by the side of the

[7].............................. .

A [8]........................... came up to him and Oliver [9].............................. to

cry. 'What's the [10]...?' the boy asked. He had

a turned-up [11].............................. and bright [12].............................. .

'I am [13].............................. and hungry and have [14]...................................

to go,' said Oliver.

'Don't [15].................................... . I'll get you [16]....................................

food,' said the boy. 'Also I [17]... an old

[18].. in London who can

[19].................................... you. His [20].. is Fagin.'

Answer the questions.

1   How did Oliver manage to eat on his way to London?

    ....

2   Where is Barnet?

    ....

3 Why did the boy ask Oliver 'What's the matter?'

....

4 Why was Oliver crying?

....

....

5 How did the boy describe Fagin?

....

People in the Story

Put the words in the correct order to make full sentences.

1 cruel Bill Sikes heavy was large with a man eyes
Bill Sikes was a large heavy man with cruel eyes.
....

2 turned-up Artful The Dodger a bright nose and eyes had

....

3 and old Oliver was years thin and eleven pale

....

4 and ugly Fagin had a face and his beard was wrinkled

....

5 Nancy wore long brightly and had hair coloured clothes

....

6 Mr gentleman Brownlow was a gold kind who wore spectacles

....

....

7   Monks was a man evil with a face as young
    as Fagin's

    ....

    ....

8   Bumble Mr long man was fat who a stick
    carried a

    ....

9   Bulls-eye was dirty was a master to dog its faithful white that

    ....

    ....

What Happened Next?

Number the sentences in the correct order to give the outline of the story.

☐ Bill Sikes took Oliver to rob a house in Chertsey.

☐ Fagin was arrested, Bill Sikes died and Monks left the country.

☐ Oliver was caught when the Dodger and Charley stole an old
    man's handkerchief.

☐ The Artful Dodger took Oliver to Fagin's rooms.

☐ Nancy told Rose Maylie that Monks wanted to harm Oliver.

☐ Bill Sikes killed Nancy.

☐ He was punished because he asked for more food.

☐ Bill Sikes and Nancy forced Oliver to go back to Fagin's rooms.

☐ At the age of eleven he ran away to London.

☐ Oliver was shot and Miss Rose Maylie took care of him.

1 Oliver was born and brought up in a workhouse.

☐ Mr Brownlow took Oliver into his house but Fagin sent Nancy
    to find him.

Choose the Verb

Complete the gaps with the correct verb form from the brackets.

Oliver [1] ....*was*......... (**was / were**) with Rose in London. Oliver [2] .... (**have told / had told**) Rose all about his life in London. He had told her about Mr Brownlow and how Mr Brownlow [3] .... (**has been / had been**) kind to him. Rose had brought Oliver to London [4] .... (**to find / for finding**) Mr Brownlow. Every day Oliver [5]............................. (**has taken / was taken**) round the streets of London in Rose's carriage. Oliver [6] .... (**is thinking / thought**) he might see Mr Brownlow or Mr Brownlow's house.

The morning after Nancy's visit, Oliver [7] .... (**has run / ran**) into Rose's room.

'I [8] .... (**have seen / had seen**) him! I have seen Mr Brownlow!' Oliver cried. 'I [9] .... (**saw / was seeing**) him going into his house.'

'Thank God,' Rose said. 'I am pleased we [10] .... (**had found / have found**) him. And he [11] .... (**can / couldn't**) help us now. I [12] .... (**visit / shall visit**) him at once.'

Dictionary: *slang*

What is *slang* language? Tick the statements that are true.

1. ☐ It is words with special meanings that certain people use.
2. ☐ It is a way of speaking politely about bad things.
3. ☐ It is words that you use in formal letters such as job applications.
4. ☐ It is street language – casual and vulgar.
5. ☐ It is language that changes quickly and is not usually put in a dictionary.

Do you know any slang words in contemporary English for *money*?

....

Phrases From the Story

Look at the examples of slang/idioms that Fagin uses in the story. Tick the correct meaning.

1 'My handkerchiefs are pretty, aren't they, Oliver? And they're all *waiting to be washed*.'
a ☐ They are dirty and need to be washed with soap and water.
b ☐ They are stolen and have identifying marks, such as the owner's initials, which must be removed before Fagin can sell them. 'Dirty' goods are stolen goods.

2 'We'll teach you to *make handkerchiefs*, Oliver. Would you like that?'
a ☐ Fagin will provide him with silk and needles and thread so he can produce handkerchiefs.
b ☐ Fagin will teach him how to steal expensive silk handkerchiefs in the street – Oliver Twist will become a pickpocket.

3 The Dodger gave Fagin two wallets. '*Very nicely made*, Dodger,' said Fagin.
a ☐ Dodger did well to steal two wallets (with money in them) and not get caught.
b ☐ The wallets are of very good quality and workmanship.

Multiple Choice 2

Tick the best answer.

1 What did Monks do with the locket Mrs Bumble had kept?
a ☐ He wore it round his neck.
b ☐ He showed it to Fagin.
c ☐ He told Mrs Corney to keep it.
d ☐ He threw it in the river.

2 How did Nancy find out about Monks' plan for Oliver?
a ☐ Fagin told Bill Sikes.
b ☐ Mrs Corney told her.
c ☐ Nancy heard Mr Bumble talking to Monks.
d ☐ Nancy heard Monks talking to Fagin.

3 Who did Nancy tell about Monks and Fagin?
a ☐ Bill Sikes.
b ☐ The police.
c ☐ Rose Maylie.
d ☐ Oliver Twist.

4 Where did Rose and Mr Brownlow meet Nancy?
a ☐ At a hotel near Fenchurch Street.
b ☐ On a platform at London Bridge Station.
c ☐ At Liverpool Street Station.
d ☐ On London Bridge.

5 How did Fagin know that Nancy had talked to Rose and
   Mr Brownlow?
a ☐ The Artful Dodger told him.
b ☐ He heard them talking.
c ☐ Charley told him.
d ☐ Bill Sikes told him.

6 What happened when Bill Sikes found out that Nancy had talked to
   Rose and Mr Brownlow?
a ☐ He ran away.
b ☐ He drowned Bulls-eye.
c ☐ He killed Fagin.
d ☐ He killed Nancy.

7 How did Mr Brownlow know Monks' father?
a ☐ He was his closest friend.
b ☐ He was his lawyer.
c ☐ He was Agnes' brother.
d ☐ He was Agnes' father.

8 What did Monks do with his father's second will?
a ☐ He asked Mr Brownlow to keep it.
b ☐ He took it to a lawyer and said it was not valid.
c ☐ He destroyed it.
d ☐ He followed the instructions carefully.

9 What did the Artful Dodger do after he was arrested?
a ☐ He told the police everything he knew.
b ☐ He kept quiet and went to prison for the rest of his life.
c ☐ He escaped and went to Australia.
d ☐ He hanged himself in prison.

10 How did Bill Sikes die?
a ☐ He drowned in a ditch.
b ☐ He shot himself.
c ☐ He hanged himself by mistake.
d ☐ Fagin hit him with a gun.

11 What happened to Monks?
a ☐ He died in prison in America.
b ☐ He sailed to Australia and disappeared.
c ☐ He vanished in Ireland.
d ☐ He was arrested and hanged.

12 Did the story end happily for Oliver Twist?
a ☐ Yes, he was adopted by Mr Brownlow.
b ☐ Yes, he was adopted by Rose Maylie and lived in Chertsey.
c ☐ Yes, he went back to the workhouse and became a beadle.
d ☐ Yes, he wrote his story and made a lot of money.

Published by Macmillan Heinemann ELT
Between Towns Road, Oxford OX4 3PP
Macmillan Heinemann ELT is an imprint of
Macmillan Publishers Limited
Companies and representatives throughout the world

PACK ISBN: 9781405076760
BOOK ISBN: 9781405073004

This retold version by Margaret Tarner for Macmillan Guided Readers
First published 1993
Design and illustration © Macmillan Publishers Limited 2002
Heinemann is a registered trademark of Reed Educational & Professional Publishing Limited
This version first published 2002

Illustrated by Kay Dixey
Cover by Ashley Pearce and Threefold Design

Printed in Malaysia

2009 2008 2007
10 9 8 7